Christmas

ISSUE

ideals

editor
Maryjane Hooper Tonn

•

managing editor
John H. Hafemeister

What is Christmas?
  It's a feeling . . .
Warm and friendly, kind and true.
It's a light that is rekindled
When the world is born anew.

Where is Christmas?
  All around us . . .
Falling snowflakes, chiming bells,
In the pleasures that surround us
And within our hearts as well.

What is Christmas?
  It's forever!
Just as long as men will show
Love and friendship and compassion,
Will the lights of Christmas glow.

©

IDEALS—Vol. 23, No. 6—November, 1966. Published Bimonthly by IDEALS PUBLISHING CO., 11315 Watertown Plank Road
Milwaukee, Wis. 53226. Second-class postage paid at Milwaukee, Wisconsin. Copyright © 1966 by IDEALS PUBLISHING CO. All
rights reserved. Title IDEALS registered U.S. Patent Office.
ONE YEAR SUBSCRIPTION—six consecutive issues as published—only $7.50
TWO YEAR SUBSCRIPTION—twelve consecutive issues as published—only $14.00
SINGLE ISSUES—only $1.50

Painting Opposite
Joan Beringer Pripps

Aida Huber Shaw

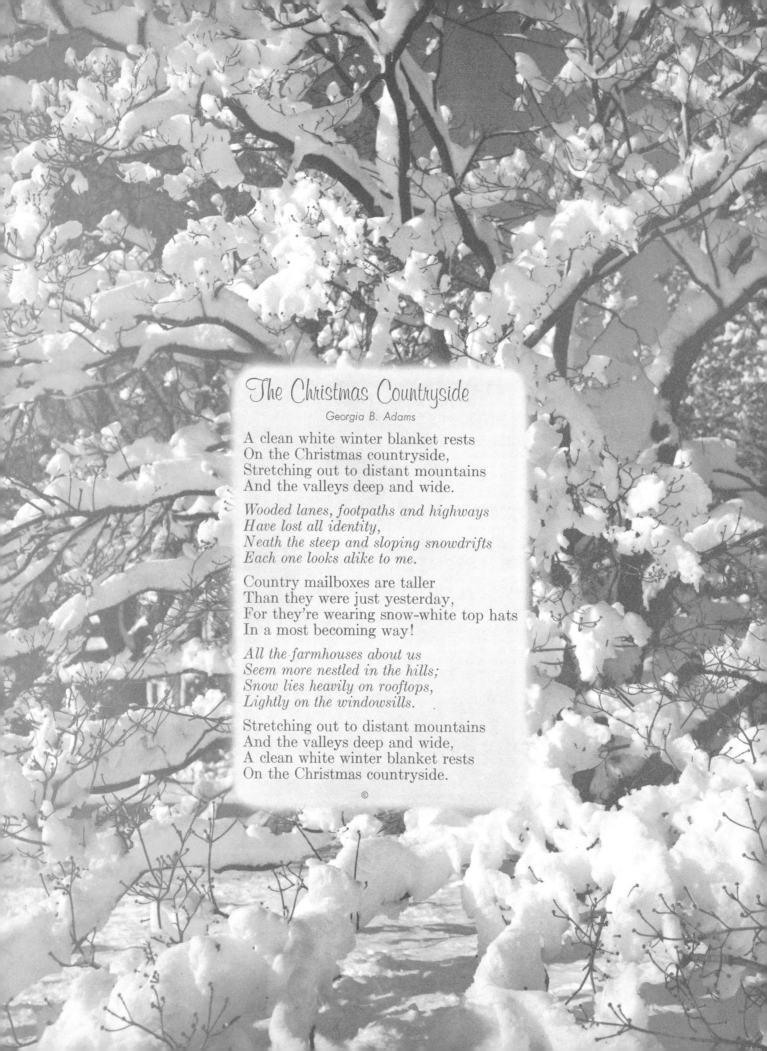

The Christmas Countryside

Georgia B. Adams

A clean white winter blanket rests
On the Christmas countryside,
Stretching out to distant mountains
And the valleys deep and wide.

*Wooded lanes, footpaths and highways
Have lost all identity,
Neath the steep and sloping snowdrifts
Each one looks alike to me.*

Country mailboxes are taller
Than they were just yesterday,
For they're wearing snow-white top hats
In a most becoming way!

*All the farmhouses about us
Seem more nestled in the hills;
Snow lies heavily on rooftops,
Lightly on the windowsills.*

Stretching out to distant mountains
And the valleys deep and wide,
A clean white winter blanket rests
On the Christmas countryside.

©

There'll Always Be Christmas

Edna Jaques

There'll always be Christmas . . . as long as a light
  Glows in the window to guide folks at night,
As long as a star in the heavens above
  Keeps shining down . . . there'll be Christmas
    and love.

There'll always be Christmas . . . as long as a tree
  Grows on a hilltop . . . as long as the sea
Breaks into foam on a white pebbled beach,
  As long as there's laughter and beautiful speech.

There'll always be Christmas . . . as long as a street
  Gives back the echo of homeward-bound feet,
And children with mittens and warm winter clothes
  Have bright eyes that sparkle and cheeks like a rose.

There'll always be Christmas . . . with holly
  and snow
  And church bells that ring in the valley below,
Shop windows lighted and doorways ajar,
  And over the housetops the glint of a star.

The cavernous length of a stocking to fill,
  A wreath on the window . . . a light on a hill,
The song of the angels, and over again
  The beautiful message . . . good will among men.

©

Sometime During Christmas

Ree Reaney

Sometime during Christmas
　As the days go rushing by,
Take time to see the Christmas lights
　Mist-haloed gainst the sky.

Sometime during Christmas
　Breathe deep the Christmas smell,
The bayberry and the piney scents,
　What welcome they foretell!

Sometime during Christmas
　When carollers are singing,
Retell the age-old story
　For which the bells are ringing.

Sometime during Christmas,
　Midst the gaiety and noise,
Take time to hear the quietness
　Of simple Christmas joys.

Sometime during Christmas
　Remember friends are near,
And feel the warmth of knowing
　Your friendship's very dear!

©

A Christmas Miracle

Beverly J. Anderson

As little towns slept peacefully
And the night was very still,
Snowflakes were softly falling
Upon valley, dale and hill.

When these little towns awakened
A miracle had been born,
The earth was robed in velvet-white,
And it was Christmas Morn.

Children gazed from snow-wrapped windows,
Filled with wonder and delight;
While squirrels and rabbits came to see
This brand-new world of white.

The trees were clothed with ermine
In patterns of frosted lace,
Though painted by an Artist's hand
Stood glistening in their place.

The earth looked like a fairyland,
The hills and valleys below,
As trees cast shadowed silhouettes
Across the gleaming snow.

Frosty icicles hung from trees
In a magical land of dreams,
And golden rays of sun shone down
On crystal brooks and streams.

This enchanting world of magic
Mantled in sparkling white
Is one of God's great miracles,
And it happened overnight!

©

Sing a Song of Christmas

Vivian Volk

O sing a song of Christmas,
A carol bright and gay,
A song as old as memory
Yet as new as today.

Sing a tender lullaby
With lilting merry air,
Words of perfect poetry
As lovely as a prayer.

O sing a song of Christmas,
And from your heart will stem
A picture pathway leading to
A town called Bethlehem.

Join chorus with the shepherds
Upon far Judean hills,
While the echo of the song
Into a far world spills.

O sing a song of Christmas,
For fear that men forget
A Child was born upon this day
And dwells amongst us yet.

Sing merrily, sing happily,
Sing softly and sing long . . .
Until the world reechoes with
This joyous Christmas song.

©

The Music of Christmas

Ruby Waters Erdelen

Again we hear the sounds of Christmastime,
Melodic church bells chime across the snow,
Young voices blend in carols' honored rhyme
Or ring with laughter under mistletoe.

We share once more the inner joy of giving
The message Christ alone was born to bring,
Of "peace on earth," the selfless way of living,
Uniting us with songs of praise to sing.

We each have special music, not always heard—
A lilt of spirit, time can never alter.
Born of song within, it knows no word
But hope and faith, or else the world would falter.

And may this wondrous music still abide
To be with you long after Christmastide.

Behold the Star

Georgia B. Adams

Behold the star embedded deep
  In eastern skies above;
It shines with brilliance all its own . . .
  Its message speaks of love.

Behold it lingers up above
  A humble cattle stall;
So still it stands where now is born
  Our Lord, the King of all.

Angelic choirs pierce velvet skies
  So lustily they sing
Of Jesus, Babe of Bethlehem,
  Our Saviour, God and King.

Draw nigh, draw nigh to Bethlehem . . .
  Come fall on bended knee
To worship Him with peasants and
  The men of high degree.

Behold the star! Behold the star!
  How brilliant is the sight.
Judea is the birthplace of
  The Christ this holy night.

©

The Glow of Christmas

Garnett Ann Schultz

May the happy glow of Christmas
Put a gladness in your heart
So you'll know the peace and goodness
That the season doth impart.
With a touch of precious holly
And some mistletoe so gay
That will add a bit of sparkle
To this extra special day.

May the lovely glow of Christmas
Fill your mind with beauty rare
As the angel voices singing
Glorify the winter air.
May you know a love unequaled
That is sent from God alone
To bring hope and faith and courage
That will bless your heart and home.

May you feel the glow of Christmas
In your every thought and dream,
That each friendly treasured greeting
Holds a happiness supreme.
For today, tomorrow and always,
'Tis my wish for you, my dear,
That the happy glow of Christmas
Lasts throughout a glad New Year.

©

Friendship

L. D. V. Dallas

What a cheerful word is *friendship*,
Especially this time of year
As we get the season's greetings
From our friends, both far and near.

It takes two to make a friendship,
Or perhaps, it's three or four,
Or we can keep right on counting
To a hundred . . . maybe more.

Friendship is not just a present
To be put upon the shelf,
The more you give, the more you gather,
Pleasing others and yourself.

Old friends are perhaps our finest
But we want the new ones, too.
A lot of love can be included
For the ones most dear to you.

Most folks know how to be friendly;
Nations too should try to be,
And thus learn that honest friendship
Is worth more than enmity.

May that wondrous Christmas message
Echo over hill and glen
Until all the world shall share it . . .
"Peace on earth, good will toward men."

©

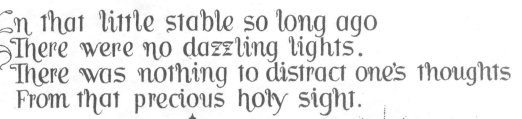

In that little stable so long ago
There were no dazzling lights.
There was nothing to distract one's thoughts
From that precious holy sight.

High above, the brilliant star
Was shining down from heaven.
And in the stillness of that moment
God's wondrous gift was given.

Shepherds came from near and far,
Their hearts were filled with love.
And watching o'er the Holy Child
Were angels from above.

The three wise men bearing gifts
At last on Him did gaze,
And as they looked in wonderment
Their lips were uttering praise.

So take a moment to recall
How this season did begin,
And make your heart a quiet stable
Where the Lord may enter in.

THE LITTLE MATCH GIRL

A long, long time ago on a bitter cold New Year's Eve, a poor little girl with bare feet was trudging along through the cold deep snow. Yes, her feet were bare because she had no real shoes. The large slippers someone had given her had been lost when she ran to get out of the way of a cart and a naughty boy ran away with them. So she was walking in the bitter, bitter cold snow, and her poor little feet were blue with cold.

In her apron she was carrying matches that she was trying to sell for a penny a box. No one had bought any from her all day long and the poor little thing was shivering and hungry; but she was afraid to go home because her cruel foster father would beat her for she had not sold even a halfpenny of matches all day long.

She looked into the bright cheerful windows of homes as she walked by . . . everyone seemed so warm and comfortable and happy, everyone except the poor little match girl. She saw a beautifully trimmed Christmas tree in one; from another came the tempting aroma of roast goose and she was so very hungry.

It was getting colder and snowing harder and was growing very dark when the little match girl huddled in a corner between two buildings to try and keep warm.

She took one little match from a box and lighted it to warm her frozen fingers. How brightly it sputtered . . . in its light she seemed to see a big warm stove. How warm and cozy it was; but when the match burned out, the stove disappeared and she was colder than ever.

She struck a second match and before her was a
big table with a glistening white tablecloth.
There was a huge roast duck and apples and cake
and warm milk, and she was so happy because she
was so terribly hungry. Then just when she was
reaching for the roast duck the match burned out,
and then she was colder and more hungry than ever.

She lighted another match and lo! there was the most
beautiful Christmas tree she had ever seen, full of
shiny toys and sparkling candles, candies and
everything nice. As she watched, the beautiful candles
began to rise higher and higher until they were
only stars in the sky . . . then one of them fell.

"That falling star means someone is dying," the
little girl said to herself. "My dear grandmother
used to tell me that."

She quickly lighted another match . . . and another . . .
then a whole handful, and in the glow, so dazzling
and bright, stood her kind and loving grandmother,
her arms outstretched.

"Grandmother!" she cried. "Please take me with
you! I know you will go away when the match
burns out just like the roast goose and the warm
stove and the Christmas tree did."

She quickly lighted the whole box of matches because
she did not want her grandmother to go. The matches
burned with a blaze that was as light as day. Her
grandmother had never seemed so beautiful, and as
she took the poor little match girl in her arms
she flew up with her in brightness and joy . . . high,
so very high where there was no cold and no hunger
and no sorrow and no matches to sell . . . for they
were in heaven.

In the morning as people passed by, they saw the
poor little girl still huddled between the buildings
with burned matches all about her.

Adapted from
Hans Christian Andersen

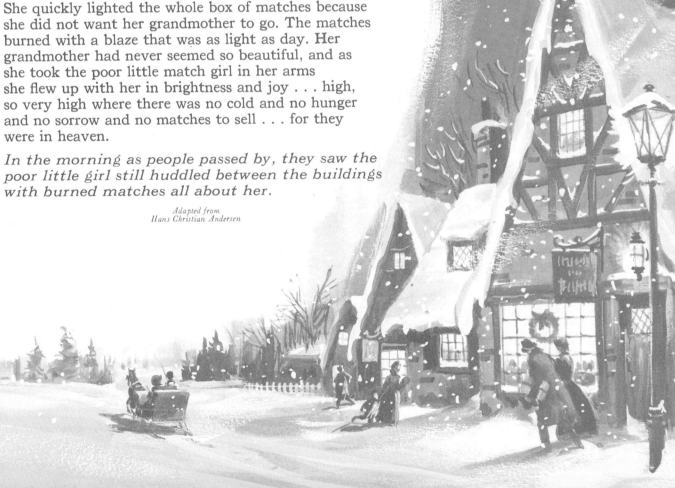

This Christmas Song

Gail Brook Burket

This Christmas song will bring to you
The melody of angel choirs,
Old carols sung across the world
And ringing bells in lofty spires.

This Christmas song will bring to you
The fragrance of the blessed myrrh
And frankincense the Magi brought,
And scent of balsam, pine and fir.

This Christmas song will bring to you
The holy beauty of the skies,
That night when men beheld the star
And glowing joy in children's eyes.

This Christmas song will bring to you
Glad tidings of God's gift to men . . .
Love manifest in Bethlehem
Illumines all believing hearts again.

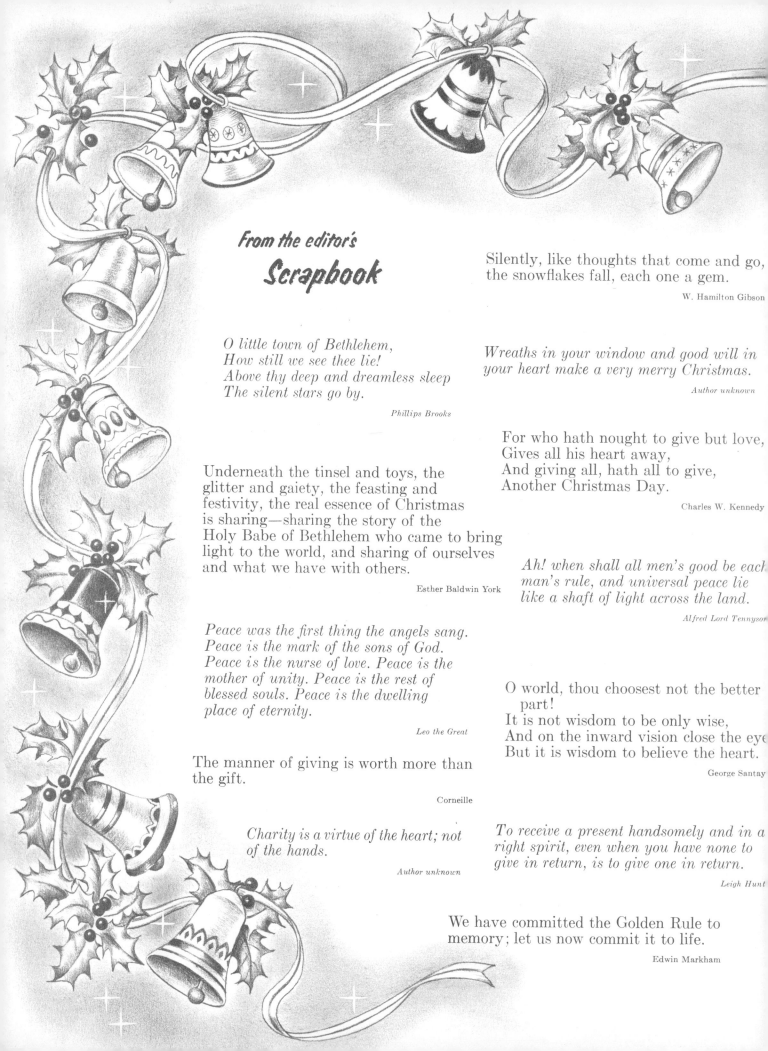

From the editor's
Scrapbook

Silently, like thoughts that come and go,
the snowflakes fall, each one a gem.

W. Hamilton Gibson

O little town of Bethlehem,
How still we see thee lie!
Above thy deep and dreamless sleep
The silent stars go by.

Phillips Brooks

Wreaths in your window and good will in
your heart make a very merry Christmas.

Author unknown

Underneath the tinsel and toys, the
glitter and gaiety, the feasting and
festivity, the real essence of Christmas
is sharing—sharing the story of the
Holy Babe of Bethlehem who came to bring
light to the world, and sharing of ourselves
and what we have with others.

Esther Baldwin York

For who hath nought to give but love,
Gives all his heart away,
And giving all, hath all to give,
Another Christmas Day.

Charles W. Kennedy

Ah! when shall all men's good be each
man's rule, and universal peace lie
like a shaft of light across the land.

Alfred Lord Tennyson

Peace was the first thing the angels sang.
Peace is the mark of the sons of God.
Peace is the nurse of love. Peace is the
mother of unity. Peace is the rest of
blessed souls. Peace is the dwelling
place of eternity.

Leo the Great

O world, thou choosest not the better
part!
It is not wisdom to be only wise,
And on the inward vision close the eyes,
But it is wisdom to believe the heart.

George Santayana

The manner of giving is worth more than
the gift.

Corneille

Charity is a virtue of the heart; not
of the hands.

Author unknown

To receive a present handsomely and in a
right spirit, even when you have none to
give in return, is to give one in return.

Leigh Hunt

We have committed the Golden Rule to
memory; let us now commit it to life.

Edwin Markham

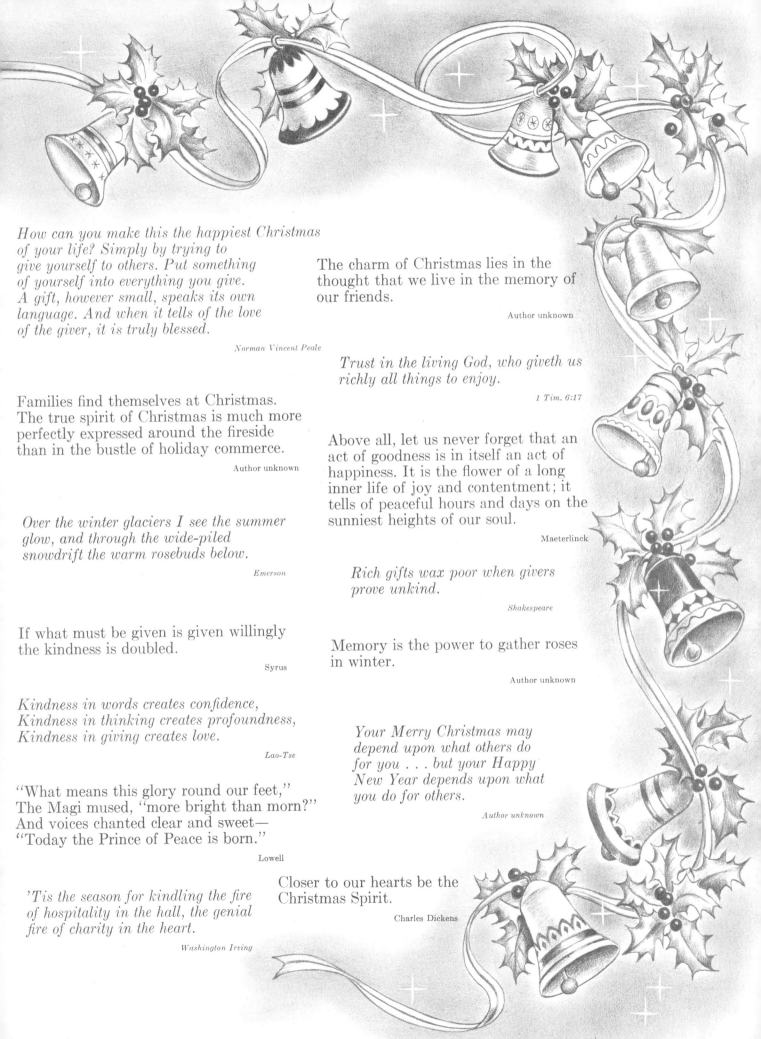

How can you make this the happiest Christmas of your life? Simply by trying to give yourself to others. Put something of yourself into everything you give. A gift, however small, speaks its own language. And when it tells of the love of the giver, it is truly blessed.

Norman Vincent Peale

Families find themselves at Christmas. The true spirit of Christmas is much more perfectly expressed around the fireside than in the bustle of holiday commerce.

Author unknown

Over the winter glaciers I see the summer glow, and through the wide-piled snowdrift the warm rosebuds below.

Emerson

If what must be given is given willingly the kindness is doubled.

Syrus

Kindness in words creates confidence, Kindness in thinking creates profoundness, Kindness in giving creates love.

Lao-Tse

"What means this glory round our feet," The Magi mused, "more bright than morn?" And voices chanted clear and sweet— "Today the Prince of Peace is born."

Lowell

'Tis the season for kindling the fire of hospitality in the hall, the genial fire of charity in the heart.

Washington Irving

The charm of Christmas lies in the thought that we live in the memory of our friends.

Author unknown

Trust in the living God, who giveth us richly all things to enjoy.

1 Tim. 6:17

Above all, let us never forget that an act of goodness is in itself an act of happiness. It is the flower of a long inner life of joy and contentment; it tells of peaceful hours and days on the sunniest heights of our soul.

Maeterlinck

Rich gifts wax poor when givers prove unkind.

Shakespeare

Memory is the power to gather roses in winter.

Author unknown

Your Merry Christmas may depend upon what others do for you . . . but your Happy New Year depends upon what you do for others.

Author unknown

Closer to our hearts be the Christmas Spirit.

Charles Dickens

...ehold, the angel of the Lord appeareth to Joseph in a dream, saying, Arise, and take the young child and his mother, and flee into Egypt, and be thou there until I bring thee word: for Herod will seek the young child to destroy him.

When he arose, he took the young child and his mother by night, and departed into Egypt:

And was there until the death of Herod: that it might be fulfilled which was spoken of the Lord by the prophet, saying, Out of Egypt have I called my son.

MATTHEW 2: 13-15

I Can Hardly Wait

Ruby Lee Mitchell

I can hardly wait till Christmas
For I'm going home again!
I won't let the weather stop me
Be there snow or sleet or rain.
I can see Mother and Father
As they go about the place
Planning for the holidays
With a smile on each dear face.

*I can see the dear old farmhouse
In the grove of tall bare trees,
With smoke drifting from the chimney,
Blowing in the wintry breeze.
And I can see the well-filled barns,
The empty fields all garnered clear.
All the homeplace seems waiting
Just to wish me Christmas cheer.*

Oh, I'm homesick, I admit it,
To see those I've loved so long.
There'll be uncles, aunts and cousins
With their laughter and their song.
How I hope there'll be a snowfall
With its beauty all unfurled.
Yes, I'm going home for Christmas...
I wouldn't miss it for the world!

©

Merry Christmas

Elizabeth Edwards

Christmas, the birthday of the Prince of
Peace, the time of homecoming, of mellowness,
of generosity, understanding and good will,
is a day of universal happiness. Our faith
is again renewed that we will yet achieve
lasting peace and brotherhood throughout
the world.

*Gay, happy laughter and the tinkle of Christmas
bells is mood music. The colors are
enchanting and triumphant from the deep
shining green of the tree to the flame colors
of the candles in the window. Bright silver,
blue and crimson sparkle everywhere from the
intriguingly wrapped packages piled beneath
a gaily decorated tree.*

Christmas has its special fragrance too . . .
the freshly baked goodies, the smell of spruce
intermingled with the delicious aroma of
roasting turkey.

*On Christmas Eve the light in our neighbor's
window shines with friendliness and good cheer.
In the heavens the evening star has a radiant
glow like the star that guided the wise men
long ago. Outside the carolers lighten your
heart as they sing, "God rest you merry,
gentlemen, let nothing you dismay."*

Ah, yes, it's Christmas everywhere with the
age-old yet ever new message, "Peace on earth,
good will to all men."

Old-Fashioned Christmas

Shirley Bryan Wright

Let's have an old-fashioned Christmas
With candles and new-fallen snow;
Let's have a bright flaming Yule log
And red stockings hung in a row.

Put up a tree in the parlor,
String it with berries and corn.
Be sure there's a light in the window,
Remembering our Saviour was born.

Hang silver bells and gay holly,
Add mistletoe just for great fun;
Hide away gifts on the highest shelves,
Remembering every loved one.

Children will whisper of Santa
And measure the chimney so wide.
At church they will sing in the program
And parents will beam in their pride.

Watch for the faces of neighbors
Made gay by the season's delight;
Give them a wave and a cheery, "Hello",
For everyone's happy and bright.

Let the house smell rich with goodies,
With cakes and a turkey and pie.
Listen for sounds in the roadways
As sleigh bells go tinkling by.

Gather around the old organ
And sing the dear carols we know . . .
Let's have an old-fashioned Christmas
Just like the ones long ago.

Bethlehem of Judea

Jessie Wilmore Murton

O little town of Bethlehem, beside the blue
   hills sleeping,
I wonder if you dream tonight? And what your
   dream may be?
Is it of gray old shepherds with white flocks
   in their keeping,
And two lone weary pilgrims come down
   from Galilee?
Do strains of angel music, from angels'
   fingers sweeping
Across their golden harp strings, stir again
   in memory?

*O little town of Bethlehem, beside the blue
   hills dreaming,
I wonder if you muse on how that glorious
   anthem rolled
Across the silent valley? How fell the strange
   star's beaming
Upon drowsy cattle, and touched the hay
   with gold?
And how a hint of radiance above a small
   head gleaming
Filled Mary's heart with wonder, and yet
   with fear untold?*

O little town of Bethlehem, beside the blue
   hills nodding,
Though centuries have left you still dreaming
   as of yore,
The shepherds' plain, the herdsmen their placid
   cattle prodding,
The ancient landmarks standing, untroubled
   as before;
Yet hearts of many peoples, the light feet and
   the plodding
Have made of you, O Bethlehem, a shrine,
   forevermore!

©

Christmas Blessings

Marian L. Moore

"Peace on earth, good will from heaven,"
　　Angels sang to all the earth
And the humble shepherds listening
　　Heard the song announce Christ's birth.

O'er the still Judean hillside
　　Rained the fire of the star,
Guiding those who saw its brilliance
　　To that wondrous gift afar.

From the East wise men came searching,
　　They had seen the heavenly light,
Bringing gifts unto the Christ Child,
　　Frankincense and gold so bright.

There beside the lowly manger
　　Knelt in homage to their King;
Laid their gifts in faithful reverence
　　To Him, for whom the bells did ring.

Years have past, but still at Christmas
　　Christ again is born once more
In the hearts of all His children
　　As the angels sang before.

Now we see the star glow brightly,
　　So it did when Christ was born . . .
May your year be filled with blessings
　　As it is this Christmas Morn!

©

Christmas of Long Ago

Earle J. Grant

Oh, for the kind of Christmas
That we had in days long ago,
With our old home in the country
Almost buried in sparkling snow.

Holly wreaths hung in the windows,
Each boasting a big bow of red;
Open fires blazed in every room
With stacks of logs in the woodshed.

The spruce tree stood in the parlor
Draped with cranberry ropes and popcorn;
Each branch was tipped with a candle
That dazzled our eyes Christmas Morn.

Spicy scents drifted from the kitchen,
Pearl-decked mistletoe crowned the door;
Loved ones gathered in from near and far
And greetings were gay above the wind's roar.

Much can be said of modern Christmases
But I treasure the ones of long ago,
At our old homestead in the country
Nestled deep in its white cloak of snow.

©

SCROOGE & MARLEY

A Christmas Carol
By Charles Dickens

Preface

...red in this ghostly little book
...t of an idea which shall not put
...he season, or with me. May it
...pleasantly and no one wish
...faithful Friend and Servant,
                                    C. D.

Stave 1
...Marley's Ghost

...There is no doubt whatever about that.
...ner. Scrooge signed it. And Scrooge's
...anything he chose to put his hand to.
...rnail.

...Of course he did. How could it be other-
...partners for I don't know how many years.
...out Old Marley's name. There it stood, years
...warehouse door: Scrooge and Marley. The firm
...e and Marley.

...a tight-fisted hand at the grindstone. Scrooge!
...ing, grasping, clutching, covetous, old
...rp as flint, from which no steel had ever struck
...et, and self-contained, and solitary as
...m froze his old features, nipped his
...stiffened his gait: made his eyes red
...shrewdly in his grating vo...
...his head, ...
...wn low temperatu...
...always about with hi...
...dog-days, and didn't thaw it one degree at C...

A Christmas Prayer

Let us pray that strength and courage abundant
be given to all who work for a world of reason
and understanding . . . That the good that lies in
every man's heart may day by day be magnified
. . . That men will come to see more clearly not
that which divides them, but that which unites
them . . . That each hour may bring us closer to
a final victory . . . Not of nation over nation,
but of man over his own evils and weaknesses
. . . That the true spirit of this Christmas
season . . . Its joy, its beauty, its hope, and
above all its abiding faith may live among
us . . . That the blessings of peace be ours:
The peace to build and grow . . . To live in
harmony and sympathy with others . . . And to
plan for the future with confidence.

Christmas in the Heart

Esther Lloyd Dauber

Have you sensed the charm of Christmas?
Have you seen the radiant star?
Heard the angels' alleluias
As they echo from afar?

*Have you felt the pulse of church bells
In the magic, mystic air?
Grasped the tenor of excitement
That each being seems to share?*

Have you glimpsed the sparkling radiance
In a little child's bright eyes?
Have you awed in silent wonder
As you gaze at star-gemmed sky?

*Have you marvelled at the beauty
Of the caroler's sweet song?
Exchanged greetings, smiles, and laughter
As you walk amid the throng?*

Have you thought about the manger
And the Babe that therein lay?
Has your heart swelled overflowing
With the love that came that day?

*Then you have the Christmas spirit,
Never let its glow depart.
Peace and love will be your measure . . .
Always Christmas in your heart.*

©

Christmas Wonder

Mamie Ozburn Odum

Nearly two thousand years of Christmases
With joy have come and gone,
Since Christ was born in Bethlehem . . .
And the wonder lingers on.

Another Christmas is with us now
To give songs to the heart,
And a special peace to all mankind
With its wonders to impart.

And as we sing loved carols,
Lift hearts to Him above,
We think of others day by day
For the rule of life is love.

Though many, many Christmases
Have filled our hearts and gone,
We have the Christ Child in our hearts . . .
And the wonder lingers on.

Painting Opposite
Frances Hook

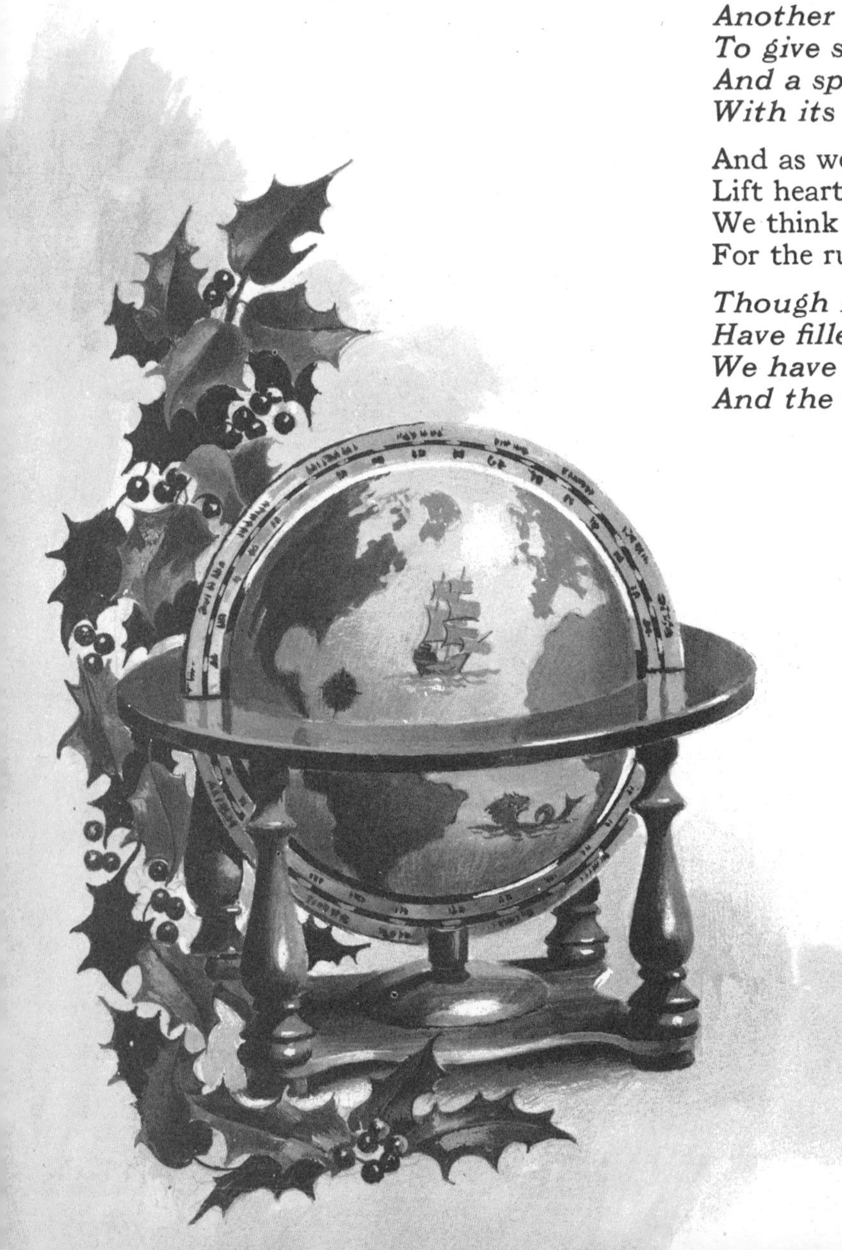

Homemade Christmas

Margaret Rorke

We love a homemade Christmas
As much as one can be,
A Christmas when we make the things
To go upon the tree;
When cookies are the ornaments
In all their varied shapes
And popcorn strung by little ones
Around the branches drapes.

We love a homemade Christmas
When everybody knows
That hours and untold patience
Were spent on wraps and bows;
And finest are the presents
Whose gay exteriors hide
Those little homemade somethings
That loved ones wrap inside.

We love a homemade Christmas
In which we all may share . . .
It casts a festive fervor
Upon the wintry air,
Which spreads to fix the season
In hearts of big and small,
Who call a homemade Christmas
The merriest of all.

©

To a Christmas Tree

Marie Hunter Dawson

Come out of the past, O Christmas tree!
Stand in the corner and let me see
Your snow-white popcorn strung on thread,
Your chains of cranberries shining red,
With bright little candles, twisted and thin,
Clamped to your branches with holders of tin;
Lemon and peppermint sticks and canes,
Homemade presents with all our names,
Clear-colored candy in animal forms,
Cookies like clowns and old-fashioned horns,
Rattles for babies and tiny dolls,
Pocket combs, mittens and popcorn balls.

Down on the floor are the dolls redressed,
The sled newly painted in Father's best,
Crocheted doilies and pillow shams,
Scarves and kerchiefs with monograms,
Slippers, perfume and bright quill pens,
Jabots edged in Valenciennes . . .
Carol singing and conversation,
Special tidbits in celebration,
Old folks happily reminiscing,
Young folks buzzing, dancing and kissing.

Come out of the past, O Christmas tree!
Stand in the corner and let me see
All that you hold in memory.

©

The·Night·before·Christmas·

'Twas the night before Christmas,
when all through the house
Not a creature was stirring,
not even a mouse;
The stockings were hung by
the chimney with care,
In the hopes that Saint Nicholas
soon would be there;

The children were nestled all
snug in their beds,
While visions of sugar-plums
danced in their heads;
And Mamma in her kerchief, and
I in my cap,
Had just settled our brains for
a long winter's nap.

Then out on the lawn there
rose such a clatter,
I sprang from my bed to see what
was the matter.
Away to the window I flew in a flash,
Tore open the shutter & threw up the sash.
The moon on the breast of the new-
fallen snow
Gave a lustre of mid-day to objects below;

When what to my wondering eyes
should appear,
But a miniature sleigh, and eight
tiny reindeer,
With a little old driver, so
lively and quick,
I knew in a moment it must
be Saint Nick.

More rapid than eagles his
coursers they came,
And he whistled and shouted
and called them by name:
"Now, Dasher! now, Dancer! now,
Prancer! now, Vixen! On, Comet!
On, Cupid! on, Donner and Blitzen!
To the top of the porch! to the top
of the wall! Now dash away,
Dash away, dash away all!"

As dry leaves that before the
wild hurricane fly,
When they meet with an obstacle,
mount to the sky,
So up to the house top the coursers
they flew, with the sleigh full of
toys and Saint Nicholas, too.
And then in a twinkling I heard
on the roof, the prancing and
Pawing of each little hoof.

As I drew in my head, and was
turning around,
Down the chimney Saint Nicholas
came with a bound.
He was dressed all in fur from
his head to his foot,
And his clothes were all tarnished
with ashes and soot;

The stump of a pipe he held
tight in his teeth,
And the smoke, it encircled his
head like a wreath.
He had a broad face and a little
round belly, that shook when
He laughed, like a bowl full of jelly.
He was chubby and plump - a
Right jolly old elf; and I laughed
when I saw him in spite of myself.

He sprang to his sleigh, to his
team gave a whistle,
And away they all flew like the
down of a thistle.
But I heard him exclaim, ere he
drove out of sight,
Merry Christmas to all, and to
all a Good Night!

Christmas Is Coming

Georgia B. Adams

The holly berries are bright red,
    They're peeping through the snow . . .
See how the flakes are sifting down
    As icy north winds blow.

The holly and the flakes hint of
    A coming Christmas Day,
Of Santa and his twelve reindeer,
    Of carols, sweet and gay;

Of fellowship with young and old,
    Of presents large and small,
Of gaily decorated trees,
    A glistening Christmas ball;

Of mistletoe and candleshine,
    Of greeting cards galore,
Of Christmas cookies, crisp and good,
    A wreath upon the door.

The icy north winds briskly blow,
    The flakes flit to and fro . . .
The holly berries, blushing red,
    Are peeping through the snow.

©

It's Christmas Stocking Time

Ann Schneider

Do you recall,
When you were small,
What gave you so much pleasure?
I remember Christmas Day;
Santa filled stockings gay
With unexpected treasure.

Limp socks in a row
Would steal the show
All through Christmas night;
While eager anticipation
And wild exhilaration
Filled our hearts with keen delight.

There they hung,
Lifeless and unsung,
Till Santa would fill them all;
To bed we went,
Our energy spent,
Waiting eagerly for his call.

Though we hardly slept,
The hours slowly crept
Till Christmas Morn arrived.
Then out of bed
With full speed ahead,
(Excitedly) we cried.

What a thrill!
Our hearts had their fill
As we spied each knobby sock.
We'll always treasure
The memory and pleasure
As around them we all would flock.

Let's keep alive
The joy we derive
From magic that Christmas can bestow.
Oh heart, never grow old
As you enfold
Memories of Christmas stockings in a row.

©

Stocking Song

Mary Mapes Dodge

Welcome, Christmas! heel and toe,
Here we wait thee in a row.
Come, good Santa Claus, we beg,
Fill us tightly, foot and leg.

Fill us quickly ere you go,
Fill us till we overflow.
That's the way! and leave us more
Heaped in piles upon the floor.

Little feet that ran all day
Twitch in dreams of merry play;
Little feet that jumped at will
Lie all pink and warm and still.

See us, how we lightly swing;
Hear us, how we try to sing.
Welcome, Christmas! heel and toe,
Come and fill us ere you go.

Here we hang till some one nimbly
Jumps with treasure down the chimney.
Bless us! how he'll tickle us . . .
Funny old St. Nicholas!

Taken from author's book
RHYMES AND JINGLES, published
by Charles Scribner's Sons

THE TWELVE DAYS OF CHRISTMAS

On the twelfth day of Christmas
My true love sent to me
Twelve drummers drumming,
Eleven pipers piping,
Ten lords a-leaping,
Nine ladies dancing,
Eight maids a-milking,
Seven swans a-swimming,
Six geese a-laying,
Five golden rings...
Four calling birds,
Three French hens,
Two turtledoves
And a partridge in a pear tree.

Illustration Opposite
Pat Thomas

Christmas Rush

Virginia Blanck Moore

"This year I simply shall not rush,"
Each Christmastime I say.
"I'll cut down on the gifts I give
And the cards I send away.
Just this once I shall forego
My usual baking spree,
And since I'm planning quietness,
Why not forget the tree?"

Each Christmastime I say these things,
But somehow every day
I see some gifts I just must buy
For dear ones far away.
The stack of cards grows by the hour . . .
Where is that recipe?
And somehow it's not Christmastime
Without a Christmas tree.

So every year I rush again,
Right up to Christmas Day . . .
And know within my inmost heart
This is the happiest way.

©

Christmas Gift

Nina Gertrude Smith

What can I wish for Christmastime
More lovely than the glow
Of mittened hands and holly cheeks
Blooming in the snow?

What can I say when all the world
Repeats one perfect story,
When soon again the bells will sing
Their glory, glory, glory.

What can I do when doors and hearts
Are opened warm and wide,
When every fragrant tree is dressed
And every bow is tied?

What can I give for Christmastime
That only I possess?
O may I give through every hour,
My time, my tenderness.

©

To a Friend at Christmas

Marion Olson

If you could come across the miles to be with me
At this wondrous Christmas season of the year,
You would hear the bells ring out across the valley,
Your heart would fill with joyful Yuletide cheer.

The snow-clad hills are lovely in the country,
The night sky filled with brightly twinkling stars,
The pond stands white and still against the north wind
And friendly cedars spread their sheltering arms.

Our hearts are filled with tender love at Christmas
As we gather in the church upon the hill.
The organ sounds and children's voices singing,
Tell us of peace on earth, to men good will.

My love goes out to you, dear friend, at Christmas . . .
I see your face within the candle's glow.
I wish you joy and peace in all your living
And may the bond of friendship stronger grow.

©

Christmas of Yesteryear

Olive Dunkelberger

When thinking of the memories
Of a Christmas long ago,
I live through every moment
With a warm and inner glow.

*Each guest was greeted at the door
With a handclasp and a smile,
Then welcomed in to share the day
In the good old-fashioned style.*

Just before the hour of dinner
Mother called, "Come, let us sing."
Everyone hurried to their places . . .
Rafters now would surely ring.

*Hymns of peace and joy unfolded,
Then with melodies of love
For the Babe who came to save us
And prepare a home above.*

Little chair and I were waiting . . .
Soon we'd hear, "O Holy Night".
Aunts and uncles, Sis and Daddy
Always sang this one just right.

*Dinner came in, hot and steaming,
To a table long and white.
Treasured china shone and
Sparkled in the candlelight.*

Grace was said by Father, then
We all did settle down
To a repast fit for any king,
But Mother had earned the crown.

*An hour later came the word
That dishes now were done.
Excitement seemed to reach its peak
For the tree and gifts and fun.*

The evergreen in red and gold
Embraced each gift supreme,
When to my knees I knelt to gaze
At a lowly manger in between.

*All this is but a memory,
A part of life so dear,
Etched forever in my heart . . .
The Christmas of yesteryear.*

©

Memory

Mary E. Richardson

Strange what memory clings to
Of Christmases gone by . . .
Tinsel, bells, and tree lights,
Spicy mincemeat pie.

Sights and sounds of Christmas,
Delicious smells and treats,
Going to Grandma's house each year
For roasted nuts and sweets.

Popcorn garlands on the tree,
Sleigh bells in the air,
"Merry Christmas!" "Same to you!"
Secrets everywhere.

Firelight warm and mistletoe,
And holly on the doors,
Singing carols in the snow,
Shopping in the stores.

Roasting turkey, pumpkin pie,
And sage and cinnamon,
Going to church on Christmas Eve
And gifts for everyone.

It isn't just the presents
Remembered from the past,
But the joy and love at Christmas
That make the memories last.

©

Ice Skating

Lolita Pinney

The skaters move like restless birds
Beneath dull pewter skies;
Their whirring blades a melody
With chords of joyful cries.

Kaleidoscope of color,
They spin and skim and glide.
Their mittened hands clasped pair by pair,
The wintry winds defied!

Skate right foot first and then the left,
Across black ice, swift flight;
When toes grow cold and fingers numb,
A bonfire lights the night.

Sweet scalding draughts of chocolate
To drink in twilight style
Reward the swooping skaters
Who pause to rest a while.

©

At Christmastime

Nancy Corinne Zuelch

In retrospect at Christmastime,
  We view the passing year.
We count our many blessings,
  Those things we hold most dear.

And as we write our Christmas cards
  Our thoughts return to those
Who make happy our remembering
  As the year draws to a close...

The merry notes they've added
  To friendship's sweet refrain,
The golden link which bears their name
  On friendship's golden chain.

They've made this year a happy one
  And as the year is done,
And we count our many blessings,
  We name each precious one.

So our greeting goes to tell them
  Those folks that we hold dear,
That their friendship means so very much
  At Christmas and all year.

©

Christmas Cards

Harriet Whipple

The cards come in with every mail
  From places far and near,
To wish me a merry Christmas
  And a happy, bright New Year.
In various shapes and sizes,
  In designs for every taste.
Some were chosen with special care
  And others just signed in haste.

There are shiny cards and parchment
  And some with sparkle glow;
There are cards with silver linings
  And some with a ribbon bow.
There are cards with red poinsettias,
  Holly and mistletoe,
With churches and covered bridges
  And carolers in the snow.

There are some with a star and manger,
  Angels, shepherds and sheep,
With wise men riding on camels
  And Bethlehem asleep.
There are cards with smiling Santas,
  With Christmas trees and bells,
Candy canes and sleighing scenes
  And deer in snowy dells.

They come with comical snowmen,
  Kittens, puppies and elves,
With holly wreaths on pretty doors
  And stockings on mantel shelves.
With piles of colored tree balls,
  And candles glowing bright,
A snowy branch with pine cones,
  A scene of Christmas night.

Some send their cards out weeks ahead
  And others just in time.
On some is a simple greeting,
  Others a verse in rhyme.
I welcome all my Christmas cards,
  They really bring me pleasure . . .
But those with a personal message
  Are the ones I always treasure.

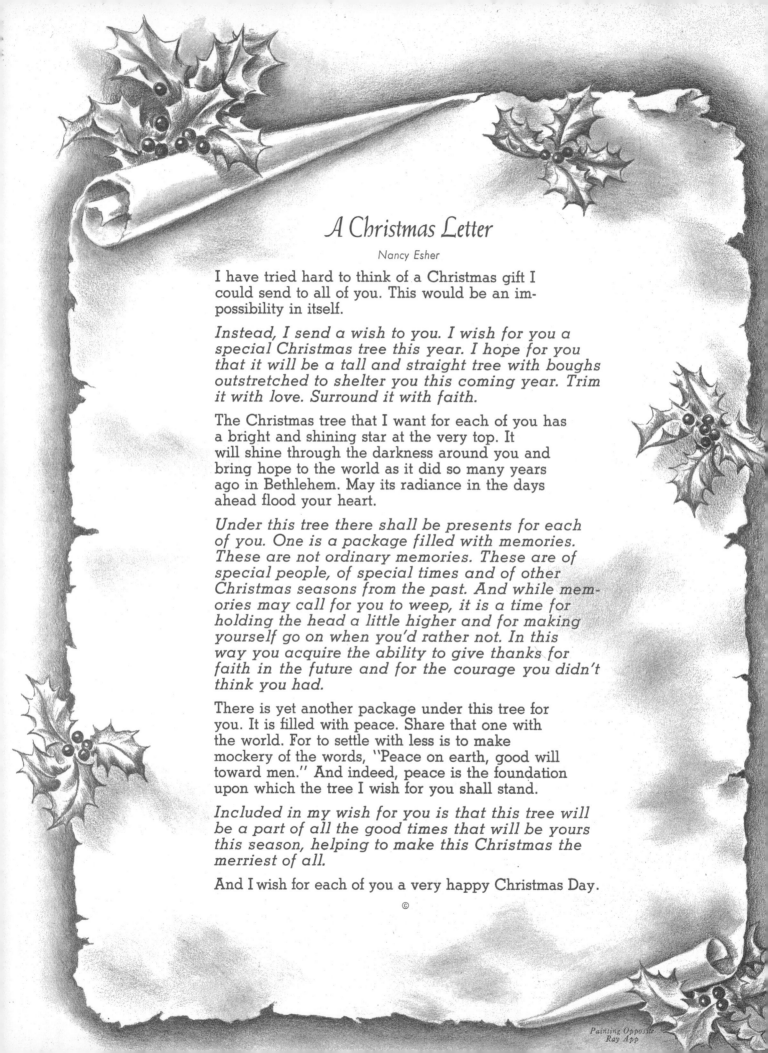

A Christmas Letter

Nancy Esher

I have tried hard to think of a Christmas gift I could send to all of you. This would be an impossibility in itself.

Instead, I send a wish to you. I wish for you a special Christmas tree this year. I hope for you that it will be a tall and straight tree with boughs outstretched to shelter you this coming year. Trim it with love. Surround it with faith.

The Christmas tree that I want for each of you has a bright and shining star at the very top. It will shine through the darkness around you and bring hope to the world as it did so many years ago in Bethlehem. May its radiance in the days ahead flood your heart.

Under this tree there shall be presents for each of you. One is a package filled with memories. These are not ordinary memories. These are of special people, of special times and of other Christmas seasons from the past. And while memories may call for you to weep, it is a time for holding the head a little higher and for making yourself go on when you'd rather not. In this way you acquire the ability to give thanks for faith in the future and for the courage you didn't think you had.

There is yet another package under this tree for you. It is filled with peace. Share that one with the world. For to settle with less is to make mockery of the words, "Peace on earth, good will toward men." And indeed, peace is the foundation upon which the tree I wish for you shall stand.

Included in my wish for you is that this tree will be a part of all the good times that will be yours this season, helping to make this Christmas the merriest of all.

And I wish for each of you a very happy Christmas Day.

©

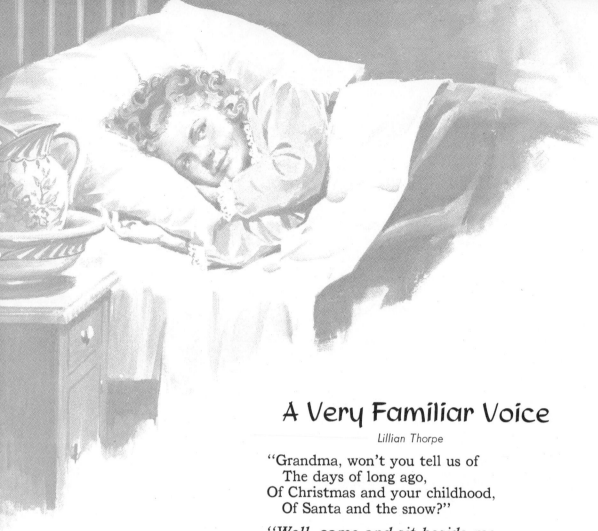

A Very Familiar Voice

Lillian Thorpe

"Grandma, won't you tell us of
  The days of long ago,
Of Christmas and your childhood,
  Of Santa and the snow?"

"Well, come and sit beside me,
  I remember, oh so well,
The Christmas tree, the presents,
  The sound of Christmas bells.

"The huge fireplace was roaring
  And winter winds did blow;
Icicles hung from the housetops,
  Everything was ice and snow.

"Mother had the shelves stacked high
  With delicious things to eat,
Cakes and pies, turkey and ham
  Made the day complete.

"I walked into the parlor
  Where Mom and Dad both sat,
And I noticed right away
  They were having quite a chat.

"I saw Mom wink and softly
  She nudged at his coat sleeve,
I remembered right away
  That it was Christmas Eve.

"I had seen the packages stacked
  Beneath the winding stairs,
And I was going to tell them
  That Santa had been there.

"But Dad, he changed the subject,
  And quickly shook his head;
Then Mom helped me with my prayers
  And tucked me into bed.

"She pulled up quilts and blankets,
  As she had done before,
And softly kissed me on the cheek
  Then closed the squeaky door.

"Somehow, I couldn't go to sleep,
  I heard voices at the tree;
Someone was helping Santa Claus . . .
  I heard them mention me.

"A very familiar voice then said,
  'I love you, Santa Claus.'
It sounded just like Mother's voice . . .
  I wonder who it was?

"The same sweet voice I used to hear
  So long, long, long ago;
The one who made our house a home . . .
  My mother's voice, I know."
  ©

Christmas Memories

Ruby Lee Mitchell

If only we could recapture
The wonderful Christmas glow
Of happiness and excitement
That only children can know.

We can remember but never
Bring back childhood's Christmas times;
The awe of Santa Claus and deer
With their jingling sleigh-bell chimes.

The wonderful smell of baking
As Mother prepared Christmas food.
Wrapped gifts, snow, holly and pine
Spiced the joyful holiday mood.

Firelight shone on the Christmas tree
And on stockings hung in a row.
Carol singing, fine dreams, suspense,
In the lamplight made bright eyes glow.

Enchanting night when angels sang,
Holy birthnight of Christ the Lord,
Such dear memories of Christmas
Are like a softly echoed chord.

©

Sing A Song of Christmas

Ann Schneider

Oh sing a song of Christmas,
Oh sing a song of toys,
Sing a song of merriment
For all the girls and boys.

Santa's in his workshop,
Busy as can be,
With his little brownies
Assisting cheerfully.

The dolls get finishing touches,
The jack-in-the-box gets his spring,
The teddy bear is now ready
And the train gets its bell to ring.

The toy horse looks so eager
To land in Santa's sleigh.
The brownies now have him finished
So he'll be ready for Christmas Day.

Santa's deft with his busy hammer,
His plane and measuring tape,
As he inspects every present
And makes sure everything is in shape.

The toy shop is busy with excitement,
As he scrutinizes each toy
And sees that it meets with approval,
Before it's wrapped for some girl or boy.

Soon all his work will be finished
In this merry North Pole town;
And we'll be marking the calendar
When Santa will be dropping around.

As this magic eve approaches
The children are good as can be.
For they want Santa to leave them
Their favorite toy under the tree.

So heed this friendly warning,
Be good in every way,
If you wish your stocking filled to the brim
On this happy Christmas Day.

©

Mrs. Santa

Rowena Califf

Old Santa is jolly,
(Now this much is true).
It's never been rumored
That he has been blue.

I like dear old Santa,
But this makes me pause . . .
How could the man manage
Without Mrs. Claus?

She looks for his glasses
While they're on his head.
She packs up the presents
While he goes to bed.

He can't find his list,
He can't find his pack,
And often it's fastened
Secure on his back.

If dolls should get restless
And frolic a bit,
If one of them whimpers
Or one should get hit,

She'd rush to it quickly
With kindness and charm.
She'd fix up its head,
Its foot or its arm.

His reindeer she pampers
With sugar and spice.
Oh, there is no doubt
Mrs. Santa is nice.

When Christmastime comes
With its snow and its holly,
If it weren't for her,
He just couldn't be jolly.

©

Jewels

Naomi I. Parks

The jewels of life are not rare stones
To be cherished and hidden away;
They are not the diamonds deep in the earth,
For which men labor each day.
They're the little things we seldom note,
That we carelessly pass by . . .
The song of the birds that herald the dawn,
The stars in the midnight sky.

They're the fragments of a robin's egg
That we find in the emerald grass,
The crystal of the dewdrops
That vanish when morn is past;
They're the silver of the moonbeams,
Too fragile for hand to hold,
Yet all of these jewels are there to see,
If we only pause to behold.

They're the perfume of the flowers
That rises like incense above,
The tender kiss of a little child
Is a jewel in a setting of love;
The precious gold of the sunshine
That flows from heaven to earth,
Reminding us of the wise men's gifts
Presented at Jesus' birth.

©

Christmas is not a time or a season but a state of mind. To cherish peace and good will, to be plenteous in mercy, is to have the real spirit of Christmas - If we think on these things there will be born in us a Savior and over us all will shine a star - sending its gleam of hope to the world.

CALVIN COOLIDGE

Calvin Harris

The Sounds of Christmas

Jane Hillsman

Christmas! The very word has a musical, magical sound, and those who have shared the beauty and the excitement and the wonder can never again be quite the same.

The sounds of Christmas . . .

The sound of footsteps on a graveled pathway . . . the postman bearing his heavy burden . . . Christmas cards that bear magic postmarks . . . and packages that show the marks of the long journey across the miles of land and sea.

The heart-stopping sound of Christmas . . . when a burst of music floats through an opened door and a fresh young voice sings the old familiar words, "I'll be home for Christmas, if only in my dreams."

The hectic, frantic sounds of the holiday shoppers who have just heard that this year Christmas will be observed on December twenty-fifth . . . the weary clerks and the exhausted customers . . . the Santa Clauses ringing their noisy bells on every corner . . . and the uniformed officers blowing their whistles in an ineffectual attempt to bring some sort of order to the chaos of the traffic tangle.

And the whispers of the children, lying wide-eyed in the dark of Christmas Eve . . . the crackle and the hiss of the Yuletide log, smoldering on the hearth.

The special sounds of Christmas . . .

The sound of carolers with overshoes and earmuffs and mittens and heavy jackets . . . their happy voices suddenly heard in the frosty air . . . carolers with rosy cheeks and slightly husky voices sharing the heart-thrilling proclamation . . . "Joy to the world, the Lord is come."

The warm and wonderful sound of a great choir . . . and the piercing sweetness of the organ, as each listening heart echoes the words . . . "O come, let us adore Him, Christ the Lord."

The unforgettable, irreplaceable sound of Christmas . . . echoing and reechoing in the hearts of men down through the ages.

But a Christian quiet falls suddenly on listening hearts.

The curious quiet of the simple shepherds beckoned by a silver star to come and find God's Blessed One.

The quiet wonder of the Christ Child lying in a manger in the little town of Bethlehem . . . God's great and perfect gift to His frail, imperfect children . . . a hushed and holy moment in the history of man.

This Christmas will soon be a page in history . . . and a new year will challenge us with its joys and its sorrows, its failures and its triumphs . . . the sounds of Christmas will fade away . . . to become only a beloved memory.

The broken tree ornaments and the tinsel and torn wrappings will be discarded.

The beautifully carved little figures in the crèche will be lovingly wrapped in tissue and put away for next year's use.

The lovely, flickering candles will have melted into nothingness.

But the quiet wonder of Christmas is ours to keep . . . as the silver star bids us come and worship . . . as our hearts return again and again to the manger in Bethlehem . . . as we share the light of the world with those who live in darkness.

Other things are limited to an hour on the clock . . . or to a day on the calendar . . . but the quiet joy of Christmas is ours forever.

©

Christmas Eve

Edgar A. Guest

Tomorrow morn she'll wake to see
The trinkets on her Christmas tree,
And find beside her little bed,
Where tenderly and soft of tread
Old Santa Claus has walked to leave,
The toys that she might still believe.

*Her stocking by the chimney place
Gives to the room a touch of grace
More beautiful than works of art
And velvet draperies can impart.
Here is a symbol of a trust
Richer than wisdom thick with dust.*

I see it through the half-swung door,
And smile to think long years before
I, too, on Christmas Eve was young
And eagerly a stocking hung
Beside the chimney just as she,
Ere knowledge stole my faith from me.

*Upstairs about her bed there seems
The peace of childhood's lovely dreams,
And I, grown old, almost forget
The truths with which I am beset.
Upon this blessed Christmas Eve
I, too, in Santa Claus believe.*

Father Says No, But...

Carolyn Callander Wright

I know it makes another mouth to feed.
  I know he'll misbehave and chew things up.
I'm told our rugs will never be the same,
  And winter is no time to train a pup.

I've heard the price of even little ones,
  Not to mention upkeep . . . simply shocking.
I also know, if I do not, just who
  Will put that pup in Junior's Christmas stocking.

©

Christmas Puppy

Oleta Larrabee

Oh! what do you buy at Christmastime
   For a boy who is about . . . so tall?
Just what can you think of at Christmastime
   That he would like best of all?

We searched through the toy stores.
   Yes, we searched through them all
To find just the right thing
   For a boy . . . 'bout that tall.

The things we saw in the windows there
   Were either too big or too small
And would never do for the gift for him . . .
   The boy just about . . . so tall.

But the gift that came on Christmas Eve
   For the boy that was just that tall,
Though tied with green bow, would fit in his hand,
   And . . . "The bestest present of all."

A little black puppy with four white feet
   And the wagglingest tail in the town
Was under and on and around and in
   And over and upside down!

The years have passed since that Christmas Eve,
   When the little black dog came to stay;
And the greeting he gives to the boy growing tall
   Gets wigglier every day!

A little black puppy with four white feet
   And the wagglingest tail in the town,
Who chews off the buckles and eats all the fudge,
   Might even tear Sis's best gown,

Is still the "bestest of presents" to get
   For a small boy . . . who'll grow six feet tall.
Just between you and me, I really do think
   That the puppy was meant for us all.

©

Along About Christmas

Lillie D. Chaffin

Along about Christmas
You'll hear it said
Small children must always go early to bed.
Strange things are happening
Which fill them with joy,
But they must not be watching . . .
Not one girl or boy!

Along about Christmas
The crispy air
Is chock-full of secrets; everywhere
It's, "Don't open the closet.
I'll get your things."
You're asked to tell wishes.
Time seems to have wings!

Along about Christmas
There's laughter and cheer
That keep it the happiest time of the year!

©

Christmas Recipe

Evy Reis

Take a bit of cheerfulness,
A pinch of laughter, too,
Next take a cup of thoughtfulness
And stir them through and through.

Add to this tranquility,
A verse of "Silent Night,"
That ever quiet we may be
When God sends His holy light.

Gently fold in some tenderness,
A handclasp or smile will do.
Perhaps it could be a fond caress,
Or a rose with a drop of dew.

Set aside a moment while you go
For spices, herbs, a scent of pine . . .
For music and fun, a candle's glow,
And a star that was the sign.

Now mix and stir and fold again,
Then add some mistletoe,
A bit of faith, and love, and then
Into the oven your cake must go.

Where warmth and affection will combine
To make this cake come true.
Garnish with happiness, truth so fine,
Enough for you and you!

Cut a piece, but save some too
For every day of the year.
Serve with a prayer for peace on earth,
And a heavenly kingdom near.

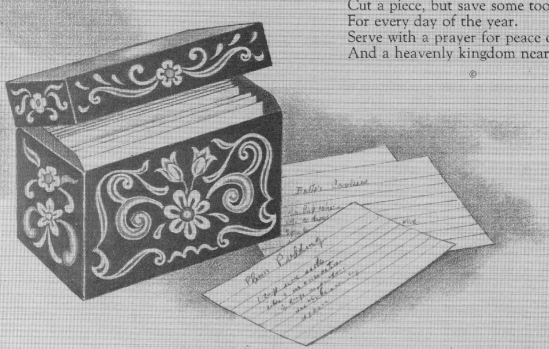

Christmas Gifts

Alberta Dredla

Of all the gifts
That Christmas brings,
The best are made
Of little things:

*Melody of carols all the year,
Cheer to friends that you hold dear;
Courage to someone else to start
Some task for which he hasn't heart;*

Thoughts for those having less than you,
Faith though the future's not in view;
Fun and laughter to go everywhere,
Kindness to show how much you care;
Strength to begin all over again,
And love to seek the best in every man.

*While other seasons come and go
And another year hurries past,
Let's give again the little things . . .
They are the gifts that last.*

A Night Like This

Reginald Holmes

This Christmas Eve the old red barn is filled
To topmost beam with crisp alfalfa hay.
The earth is locked in winter's icy grasp,
But here, the fragrance of a bright June day.

An air of hushed expectancy prevails.
The evening star hangs low in moonlit skies.
A newborn calf stands at its mother's side
And views a newfound world with wondering eyes.

The sheep have piled their fleecy whiteness here
To form a contrast with the drab gray walls;
They raise their heads and silently protest
As horses softly neigh in nearby stalls.

No man alive dare say their vision soars
No higher than those wooded pasture bars.
Who knows, but long ago they scanned the skies
And saw the brilliance of that star of stars.

But this I surely know . . . a miracle
Will never be to them a strange new thing;
For on a night like this in Bethlehem
Their forebears watched the advent of the King.

©

Would You Follow?

Helen E. Middleton

How many would follow the star tonight
If it shone past the Milky Way,
Leave comfortable homes and follow it still
Over the hills and away?

*How many would open their doors tonight
For a weary and shabby pair,
Make room at hearths for a Stranger-Child
Though the Infant be wondrous fair?*

How many would give of their goods tonight,
The best they possess and more,
For their faith in a star and an angel choir
And a King forevermore?

*We censure the folk of a bygone time
For indifference to Mary's plight.
How many would do any better now?
Would you follow the star tonight?*

©

The Star of Christmas

Quitillia B. Russell

I do not want a roof this Christmas night.
I long to walk the open field, or lie
Face upward on a hill and watch the sky
Sparkling with silver, and to know
That one night long ago
The same stars, with the same Hand guiding them,
Shone down on Bethlehem.

The roof shuts out the stars. It drugs with sleep.
I want to be a shepherd boy of white sheep
Out on the hills, and for their sake
To keep awake.
Then I would see the grandeur of the sky,
The rapture of the slow stars marching by,
The near one bright, the far ones dim,
But speaking every one of them of Him.

That's why I do not want a roof this Christmas night.
But from the hill, if I should hasten down,
Where shine the lights in simple home or town,
I think that I should find the Christ Child there
Under the star, somewhere.
Faith or fancy . . . call it what you will,
The Star of Christmas guides me to Him still.

©

The Way To See Christmas

Ruth Carter

The way to see Christmas is through
   a child's eyes,
As she opens with rapture some
   hidden surprise;
As she looks at the tree with its
   lights blue and gold;
As she climbs on your lap, knowing
   arms will enfold.

*Someone plays Christmas carols,
   you listen, you rock;
Save the music, no sound but the
   ticktock of clock.*

In spite of your worries, in spite
   of your grief,
'Tis the child and his wonder, his
   trusting belief
Renewing your faith of that Child
   long ago
Reflected in your child, God's gift
   to bestow.

*Rock away, rock away, loveliness
   keep
Of the child on your shoulder,
   fallen asleep.*

So the way to see Christmas, if you
   would be wise
Is to share it with children, see
   joy in their eyes!
For the world is a weary world,
   troubles increase;
But the child who is loved . . . it is
   she who has peace.

©
Reprinted from The P.E.O. RECORD

*Painting Opposite
John Walter*

Poem for a Winter Night

Grace V. Watkins

In every winter I must know
The healing loveliness of snow,
Must see across the quiet night
A hushed immensity of white;
And on the dark blue calendar
Of sky, a silent-shining star.
How wonderful it is that I,
A cousin to the earth and sky,
Should look on snow and star and be
A part of God's infinity!

©

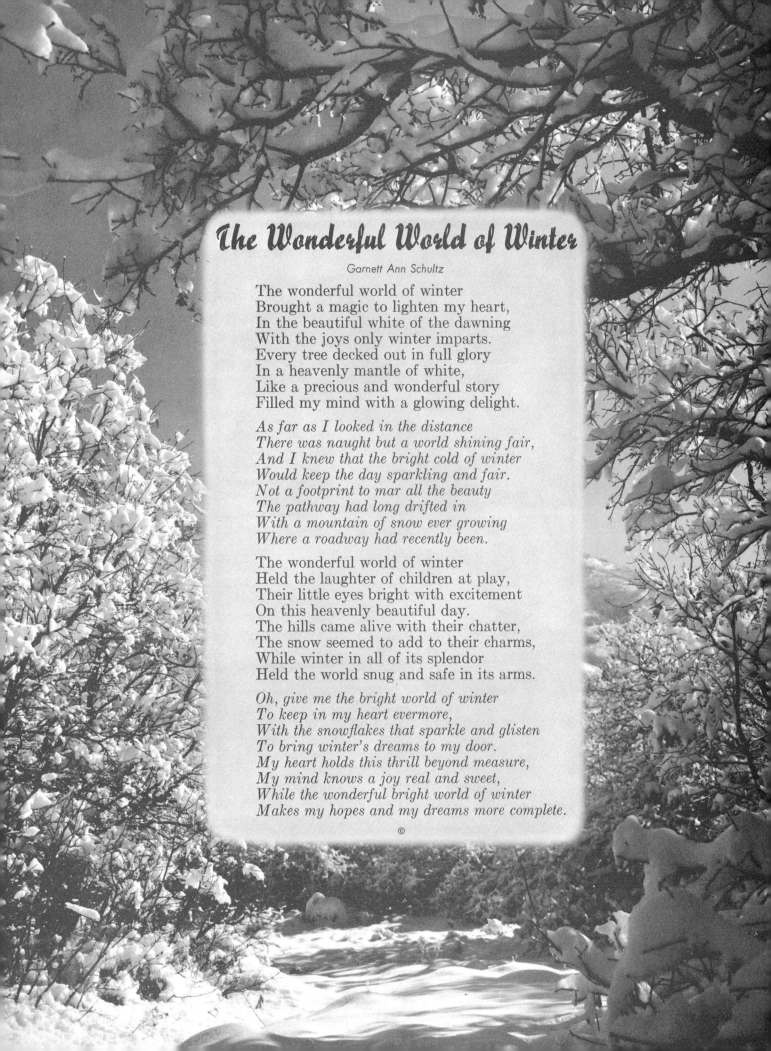

The Wonderful World of Winter

Garnett Ann Schultz

The wonderful world of winter
Brought a magic to lighten my heart,
In the beautiful white of the dawning
With the joys only winter imparts.
Every tree decked out in full glory
In a heavenly mantle of white,
Like a precious and wonderful story
Filled my mind with a glowing delight.

As far as I looked in the distance
There was naught but a world shining fair,
And I knew that the bright cold of winter
Would keep the day sparkling and fair.
Not a footprint to mar all the beauty
The pathway had long drifted in
With a mountain of snow ever growing
Where a roadway had recently been.

The wonderful world of winter
Held the laughter of children at play,
Their little eyes bright with excitement
On this heavenly beautiful day.
The hills came alive with their chatter,
The snow seemed to add to their charms,
While winter in all of its splendor
Held the world snug and safe in its arms.

Oh, give me the bright world of winter
To keep in my heart evermore,
With the snowflakes that sparkle and glisten
To bring winter's dreams to my door.
My heart holds this thrill beyond measure,
My mind knows a joy real and sweet,
While the wonderful bright world of winter
Makes my hopes and my dreams more complete.

©

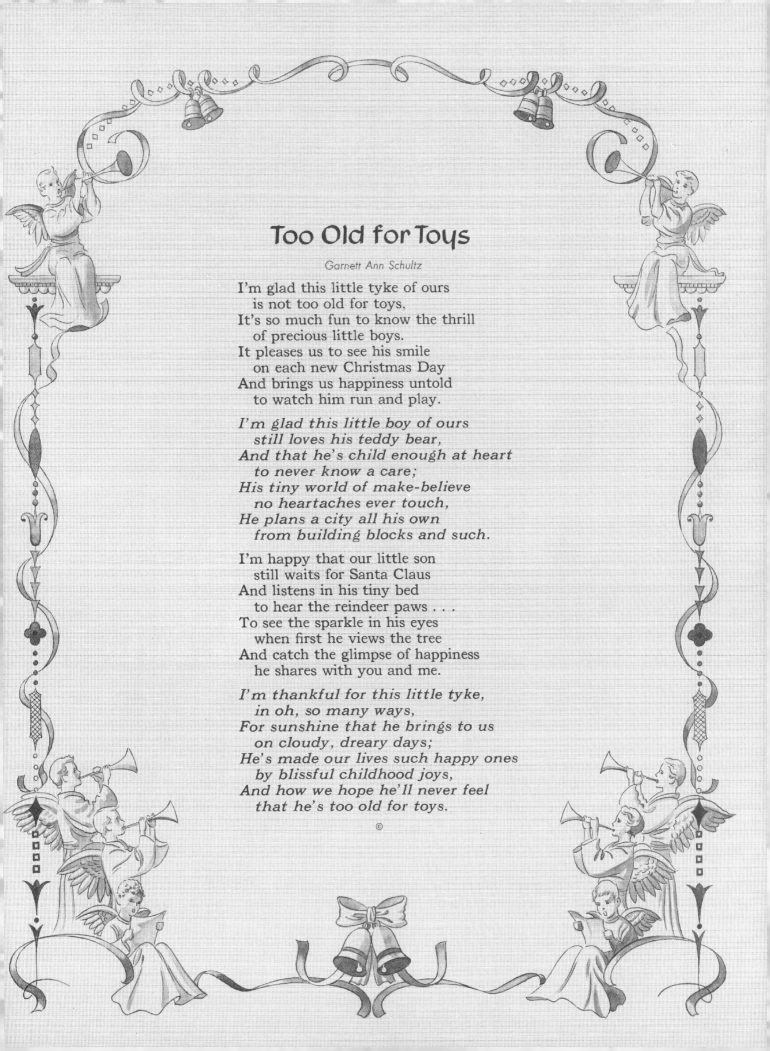

Too Old for Toys

Garnett Ann Schultz

I'm glad this little tyke of ours
　is not too old for toys,
It's so much fun to know the thrill
　of precious little boys.
It pleases us to see his smile
　on each new Christmas Day
And brings us happiness untold
　to watch him run and play.

*I'm glad this little boy of ours
　still loves his teddy bear,
And that he's child enough at heart
　to never know a care;
His tiny world of make-believe
　no heartaches ever touch,
He plans a city all his own
　from building blocks and such.*

I'm happy that our little son
　still waits for Santa Claus
And listens in his tiny bed
　to hear the reindeer paws . . .
To see the sparkle in his eyes
　when first he views the tree
And catch the glimpse of happiness
　he shares with you and me.

*I'm thankful for this little tyke,
　in oh, so many ways,
For sunshine that he brings to us
　on cloudy, dreary days;
He's made our lives such happy ones
　by blissful childhood joys,
And how we hope he'll never feel
　that he's too old for toys.*

Peace, Noel

Jean Masamba

Peace, brotherhood . . .
This is the sound of Noel.

Peace, renewing . . .
This is the spirit of Noel.

Peace, reconciliation . . .
This is the symbol of Noel.

Peace, love . . .
This is the hymn of Noel.

Peace, serving . . .
This is the joy of Noel.

Peace, prayer . . .
This is the gift of Noel.

Peace, rebirth . . .
This is the eternity of Noel.

Peace, faith . . .
A new era—this is Noel.

©

Christmas

Isabel Sanderson

Of course the world cannot stand still,
Nor birds pause in their flight,
But oh, if we could hold at will
This magic of delight!

For Christmastide, since time began,
Has filled all hearts on earth
With friendship for each fellowman . . .
The essence of Christ's birth.

©

CHRISTMAS WINDOWS

Alice Kennelly Roberts

There are dreams in Christmas windows,
Symbols of love and joy,
And hopes of happy childhood
For some little girl or boy.

There's a vision of chubby fingers
And arms reaching out to hold;
A smile that is wreathed in dimples,
Surpassing its worth in gold.

Yes, dreams are in Christmas windows
But the giver himself must share,
Must join in the love of giving,
Or the gift becomes plain and bare.

And so, as the snowflakes glisten
In our Christmas world apart,
The dreams in a bright shop window
Are Christmas in someone's heart!

©

Christmastime

Irene Taylor

The snow falls like feathers
So fluffy and white,
It lies on the ground
At a good sledding height.

Oh, bring out the boots
Coats, gloves and caps,
Button up buttons
And fasten down flaps.

Out with the sleds from their
Months stored away,
Off to the slopes
Where there's frolic and play.

Snowballs are ready,
"That was a good throw!"
Snowmen and sledding . . .
Oh, beautiful snow.

Home late for supper,
Chilled through from wet clothes,
How lovely are memories
Of Christmastime snows.

©

Now and Then

Mary A. Selden

Think about the wintertime
And what it means to you;
Then turn your thoughts to childhood days,
To things you used to do.

Lean against the icy winds
In your heavy clothes;
Break off brittle icicles . . .
Strike a fencing pose.

Catch some snowflakes in your hand,
Taste their frosty lace;
Brush a pair of angel wings,
Tramp a circle chase.

Coasting down the nearest hill,
Steer your homemade sled;
Skate around a tiny pond
With flailing arms outspread.

Build a snowman, build a fort
With snowballs stacked in mounds;
Clear a space to slide upon,
Play at "fox and hounds."

Run for home to help with chores,
Hear the old clock chime . . .
Live again and know again
The joys of wintertime.

©

Snow Storm

LaVerne P. Larson

All night the crystal flakes of white
Fell from a brooding sky
And covered forest and field and lane
To North Wind's lullaby.

It seemed that everything in sight
Took on a magic glow,
Bedecked in sparkling splendor
Of winter's pure white snow.

The roofs of all the houses
Looked like an ice cream treat,
While forest and field and lane
Were tucked in snug and neat.

There was a holy silence
Through the busy streets of town,
As all the merry snowflakes
Wove a wondrous diamond gown.

The snowstorm slowly ebbed and then
Small folks came out to play,
To make the most of Winter's gift
Before it went away.

©

Old and New

Farewell, Old Year!
With goodness crowned
A hand divine hath set thy bound.

Welcome, New Year,
Which shall bring
Fresh blessings from my God and King!

The old we leave without a tear,
The new we hail without a fear.
Because,
I know that o'er it all
Rules He who notes the sparrow's fall.

Author unknown

A Prayer for the New Year

May it be Thy will,
Our God and God of our fathers,
That this coming year be unto all Thy people:
    A year of plenty,
    A year of blessings,
    A year of assembly in Thy sanctuary,
A year of happy life from Thee,
A year of dew and rain and warmth,
A year in which Thou wilt bless our bread and water,
    A year in which Thy mercies will be moved toward us,
    A year of peace and tranquility in which Thou
    wilt set a blessing upon the work of our hands.

Ancient Hebrew Prayer

JANUARY · 1967
1
SUNDAY

Flower of the Snow

Shirley Sallay

I know a spot where holly grows
In splendor bright and gay,
It tells a tale of Christmas,
And days of tinsel and sleigh.

Green leaves waxed well by nature
To an emerald-tinted hue,
With scarlet berries in clusters
There hidden from our view.

And when the time is exactly right,
With basket on my arm,
I go to the spot where holly grows
On the corner of our farm . . .

To gather for His birthday
A bouquet, the best by far . . .
A wonderful gift from nature
To place beneath His star.

©

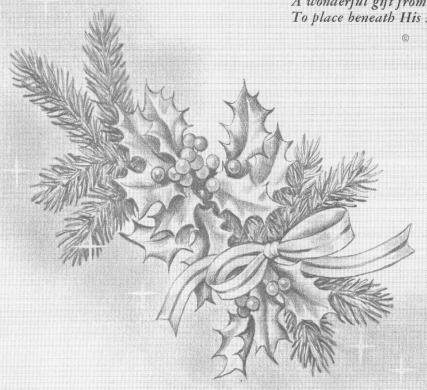

Lasting Memories

Winnie Barnett

Once again we fondle trinkets
Before they're carefully stored away
And relive the glorious moments
Of the Christmas holiday.

*There's a bright and shining angel
Stored with balls from off the tree,
The manger scene and oft-used candles
That gave a light for all to see.*

The holly wreath and glittering tinsel
Which added to our Christmas cheer
Are put within a box containing
Wrappings, ribbons, till next year.

*We reread the cherished greetings
From our loved ones, near and far,
And pray their paths may all be guided
By the Babe and Christmas star.*

Then as the tree is taken down
A sudden sadness does descend,
Yet in our hearts we know full well
Its glow and warmth will never end.

*So we tie some bread and suet on,
Then place it out of doors
And watch the feast of feathered friends
And scampering squirrels by the score.*

Yes, Christmas treasures wrapped in tissue
And caressingly packed away
Will leave a lovely lasting memory
Till another Christmas Day!

©

*Painting Opposite
Joan Beringer Pripps*

You are invited to enjoy Ideals the year 'round

*Enter an Ideals subscription
for yourself and for loved ones
at Christmastime*

As the name implies, IDEALS are issues of clean, wholesome, old-fashioned American ideals—homey philosophy—poetry—art—music—inspiration—neighborliness—things many of us have overlooked during these busy days.

An IDEALS SUBSCRIPTION brings a new, exquisitely beautiful issue, into your home SIX TIMES during the year. The colorful seasons of the year, the significant holidays, the meaningful themes convey inspiration and reading pleasure as each issue comes to you. Vibrantly illustrated and artistically presented, IDEALS contains NO ADVERTISING.

Each IDEALS issue, published about every sixty days, consists of 100 lovely and colorful pages . . . unexcelled artistry, reproduced and printed according to the highest degree of publishing excellence, is reflected in every issue of IDEALS. The deep tone heavy art cover has a permanent plastic coating to protect and enhance its beauty.

A perfect Christmas present for FAMILY and FRIENDS, a yearly GIFT SUB-SCRIPTION to a series of IDEALS enriches the lives of those whom you love.

A lovely gift announcement will be sent to the recipient of your GIFT SUBSCRIP-TION to herald your thoughtfulness at Christmas and throughout the year with a ONE YEAR SUBSCRIPTION to a series of IDEALS.

An IDEALS subscription is so inexpensive—only $7.50—just indicate the issue with which you want your own—and your gift subscriptions to begin. Order now—each new issue, as published, will be reserved for mailing to you and to those to whom your gift subscription will be sent. THANKSGIVING IDEALS and CHRISTMAS IDEALS will be mailed to arrive at the appropriate time for the holiday.

Subscription Plans

ONE YEAR 6 issues *$7.50* . . . . **TWO YEAR 12 issues** *$14.00*

PAY-AS-YOU-READ-PLAN. An easy payment plan for you. Upon receipt of your Pay-As-You-Read-Plan order, the current issue of IDEALS is mailed to you along with an invoice for $1.50. Your payment of $1.50 by return mail makes you eligible for the next IDEALS issue automatically. You will continue to receive about every 60 days a new IDEALS issue until you cancel your Pay-As-You-Read-Plan Subscription. You may cancel, of course, at any time simply by notifying us.

The Following Ideals Issues Will Be Delivered to Subscribers

CHRISTMAS IDEALS
(Nov. 1, 1966)

The religious significance of Christmas—the excitement of children on Christmas morn, memories of long ago, portrayed in inspiring art and lovely illustration.

EASTER IDEALS
(Mar. 1, 1967)

The inspiration of Easter, the bursting of springtime, the true meaning and sacredness of the Easter Season—presented in poetry, prose and beautiful art reproductions.

SCENIC IDEALS
(July 1, 1967)

A most interesting and richly illustrated book depicting the scenic beauty of our wonderful country—the wonders of nature—colorful pages of the great outdoors.

COUNTRY IDEALS
(Jan. 1, 1967)

The artistic portrayal of nature's unspoiled beauty—wholesome pleasure of family togetherness—doing for others—life's friendships.

FAMILY IDEALS
(May 1, 1967)

Warm reflections of home—memories of bygone days—the unity of family love presented in a most artistic way in a lovely issue the whole family will enjoy.

THANKSGIVING IDEALS
(Sept. 1, 1967)

Gorgeous scenes of AUTUMN, vivid color photographic and art illustrations—the festival harvest season—memories of school days portrayed in this annual holiday issue.

$150 each

$150 each

Size 8½ x 11 inches

Colorful Past Ideals Issues You'll Enjoy

Cellophaned Art Covers

NEIGHBORLY IDEALS 1966

Neighborhood coffee time . . . a welcome supper . . . our neighbors' lasting friendships . . . the gathering place on the large front porch . . . are recalled happily in this most unique and treasured issue.

FIRESIDE IDEALS 1965

Prose and poetry bring reminiscences of warming frosted toes at a skating pond bonfire—story telling around the blazing stove at the country store—and the coziness of your own hearthside.

RURAL IDEALS 1966

Quiet, peaceful country roads . . . the beauty of colorful wildflowers . . . a country church nestled among green rolling hills . . . a country fair are just a few of the interesting themes presented in this lovely issue.

THANKSGIVING IDEALS 1965

The festive harvest—Halloween—back to school—and the deep significance of Thanksgiving Day presented colorfully in prose, poetry and colorful art reproductions.

CHRISTMAS IDEALS 1963

The true spirit of this holy season—the festivities—the joys of Christmas—the melodious Christmas songs . . . are reflected artistically and reverently throughout this very

CHILDREN'S IDEALS 1966

The joys and delights of carefree youth, the happiness of children, the excitement of summer days, are expressed in prose, poetry and beautiful art and photographic reproductions for the entire family's enjoyment.

THANKSGIVING IDEALS 1964

Contains 100 pages of prose and poetry reflecting the joys of the bountiful harvest season. Breathtaking reproductions of the colorful countryside, the family reunion on Thanksgiving Day, artistically presented in this beautiful issue.

CHRISTMAS IDEALS 1964

The religious spirit of the true Christmas and the cherished memories of this happy season are poetically and artistically awakened in

$150 each

100 lovely pages

Your Personal Order

Important—Items checked here will be sent directly to you at the address below.

In order to process and deliver your order as rapidly as possible write or type your proper Zip Code in the space provided. The Postal Department soon will make Zip Codes mandatory on all mailing addresses.

*YOUR ZIP CODE IS NECESSARY

Please

YOUR NAME

ADDRESS

CITY

STATE   ZIP CODE

Please print clearly

ITEM	QUANTITY	AMOUNT
CHRISTMAS IDEALS @ $1.50		
THANKSGIVING IDEALS 1966 @ $1.50		
COUNTRY IDEALS (Available Jan. 1, 1967) @ $1.50		
RURAL IDEALS 1966 @ $1.50		
CHILDREN'S IDEALS 1966 @ $1.50		
NEIGHBORLY IDEALS 1966 @ $1.50		
FIRESIDE IDEALS 1965 @ $1.50		
1 YEAR SUBSCRIPTION* (6 consecutive IDEALS issues) @ $7.50		
2 YEAR SUBSCRIPTION* (12 consecutive IDEALS issues) @ $14.00		
PAY AS YOU READ SUBSCRIPTION* (1 copy each IDEALS issue with invoice) @ $1.50		
TOTAL COLUMN 1	$	

Foreign Postage   (Except U.S. and Possessions, Canada and Mexico)

One Year Subscription	Add $1.00
Two Year Subscription	Add $2.00
IDEALS BINDER	Add $ .50
Single IDEALS	Add $ .15
Each Single Hardbound Book	Add $ .15
Each Set of Prints	Add $ .14

ideals PUBLISHING CO., P.O. BOX 1101, MILWAUKEE, WIS. 53201

Your Gift Order

Please indicate zip code in order that we may process and deliver this order as rapidly as possible.

To:

ADDRESS

CITY   *   STATE   ZIP CODE

Please print clearly

from

ITEM	QUANTITY	AMOUNT
CHRISTMAS IDEALS @ $1.50		
THANKSGIVING IDEALS 1966 @ $1.50		
COUNTRY IDEALS (Available Jan. 1, 1967) @ $1.50		
RURAL IDEALS 1966 @ $1.50		
CHILDREN'S IDEALS 1966 @ $1.50		
NEIGHBORLY IDEALS 1966 @ $1.50		
FIRESIDE IDEALS 1965 @ $1.50		
1 YEAR SUBSCRIPTION* (6 consecutive IDEALS issues) @ $7.50		
2 YEAR SUBSCRIPTION* (12 consecutive IDEALS issues) @ $14.00		
TOTAL COLUMN 2	$	

Important Note—

AFTER you have entered and checked your entire order in the spaces provided—please tally your order here to assure accuracy of your remittance.

*All subscriptions will begin with CHRISTMAS IDEALS unless otherwise requested.

Your Gift Order

Please indicate zip code in order that we may process and deliver this order as rapidly as possible.

To:

ADDRESS

CITY   *   STATE   ZIP CODE

Please print clearly

from

ITEM	QUANTITY	AMOUNT
CHRISTMAS IDEALS @ $1.50		
THANKSGIVING IDEALS 1966 @ $1.50		
COUNTRY IDEALS (Available Jan. 1, 1967) @ $1.50		
RURAL IDEALS 1966 @ $1.50		
CHILDREN'S IDEALS 1966 @ $1.50		
NEIGHBORLY IDEALS 1966 @ $1.50		
FIRESIDE IDEALS 1965 @ $1.50		
1 YEAR SUBSCRIPTION* (6 consecutive IDEALS issues) @ $7.50		
2 YEAR SUBSCRIPTION* (12 consecutive IDEALS issues) @ $14.00		
TOTAL COLUMN 3		

POSTAGE (ADD FOREIGN POSTAGE ONLY)

GRAND TOTAL COLUMNS 1-2-3

Add 7% for Canadian Currency Exchange. The Postal Authorities strongly recommend that you send your remittance by check or money order—NO CASH or STAMPS.

I Enclose my ☐ Check ☐ Money Order

THANK YOU!

If you have friends or relatives who would be interested in receiving a catalog of Ideals Publications, please list their names below.

NAME _____
Please print clearly

ADDRESS _____

CITY _____

STATE _____ ZIP CODE _____

NAME _____
Please print clearly

ADDRESS _____

CITY _____

STATE _____ ZIP CODE _____

NAME _____
Please print clearly

ADDRESS _____

CITY _____

STATE _____ ZIP CODE _____

from _____

_____

_____ ( ) _____
ZIP CODE

ideals PUBLISHING CO.

P.O. BOX 1101

MILWAUKEE, WIS. 53201

FOLD HERE FIRST

FOLD SIDE FLAPS FIRST — THEN FOLD HERE

For Office Use Only			TYPE	AMT
ENTRD			IDEALS	
REMTC			Subs	
	C	K	Mo	Binders	
	1 / 66		Prints	
ACKD			P.A.Y.R.	
Checked for Accuracy			Postage	
			Total	

20

FOLD HERE FIRST

FOLD SIDE FLAPS FIRST
When properly sealed with the above gummed flap this envelope and its contents will travel safely through the mail.
NO ADDITIONAL SEALING MATERIAL IS NECESSARY

If you desire additional gift copies or subscriptions sent to your friends—attach a separate list and they will be handled promptly and carefully for you.

For all occasions—give a distinctive gift instead of an expensive one